Snowdrops
in the
Winter

An anthology of heartfelt,
moving and inspirational poems

By

Candice Flower

© Candice Flower 2020

All rights reserved.

No part of this publication may be reproduced, distributed or transmitted, in any form or by any means, including photocopying, recording or other electronic or mechanical methods, without the express permission of the publisher, except in the case of brief quotations embodied in reviews and certain other non-commercial uses permitted by copyright law.

First edition 2020

ISBN 9798648411036

In loving memory of
my dearest mother Jean Ann.

Contents

Humpty Dumpty (First person) 1

Humpty Dumpty (Second person) 3

Humpty Dumpty (Third person) 5

Happy Days 8

A Story to Be Told 9

Disturbed Silence 12

Autumn 14

The Telephone 15

May Day 17

Walking Through a City 19

Me and You Should Never Be Apart 21

A Life So Free 22

Be Bee Be 23

Root Top Songs 24

What I Really Dislike 25

Shine a Light 27

Wasted Wealth...29

Together We Can 30

A Love Gone Cold 32

She Lives On Though She Has Gone 34

Oh Happy Day..36

Mixed Morning...38

Mr Fish..39

Up From the Soil..40

My Struggle 42

For My Mom on Her Birthday 44

No Body, No Pain 47

Heaven's Gain 48

Magnificent Mountains...49

The Deep Secret 51

Delight Land 53

Night...54

What a Day...55

In Peace 57

Family	58
Those We Love	59
I Tried	60
Mom in Heaven	62
Not You, Not Me	63
A New Season	66
A New Day	67
As We Are	68
Time	69
The Still	70
Falling Silence	71
Happy Days	72
Sweets	73
The Last Day	74
Snowflakes	75
The Town	76
Tired	78
Misfits	80
A Formed Life	83
Angel of Light	86

The Rose 88

So Beautiful To Me 90

As You Sleep 93

Onwards You Go 95

Your Light 97

Preface

*F*rom being a fully able-bodied and functional nurse in the intensity of a hospital ward to being confined to a wheelchair – never did I think I would be publishing my very own poetry book.

Lying in the darkness and despair of uncertainty of recovery day after day post a traumatic brain injury, unable to write, walk or even recall my name most days; with unimaginable suffering, loneliness and pain – I could not imagine what my life would be like nor did I know how I was going to survive let alone thrive.

Half a decade down the line remaining with significant disabilities, I have been able to turn to poetry to express myself. Not just in times of happiness, frustration and emotional pain but in noticing the world, people and relationships. Learning to juggle what life now means for me and navigating through this new path of relating to the world, poetry has helped me capture this journey and also notice the world in a new light.

From happy and light-hearted poems to poems from within the cry of my heart, this compilation will carry the reader through many relatable moments.

I have dedicated this book to my late mother who taught me much of the value and meaning of life. I have included fifty-nine poems – the age she was when she passed away.

I owe the making of this book to the invaluable support of and from Headway Nottingham who have brought out new strengths and abilities in me I did not know I have.

From feeling like I was a no-one, they have helped me to see I am still a someone.

Humpty Dumpty

(First person)

I am a squirrel in a tree
Sitting up so high & as happy as can be
With a bird and a song
The day looking so lovely & long

Oh what chaos I now see below
Shouts and screams, I hear a bellow
A man, no an egg, was sitting so tall
Oh but now he has fallen off a wall!

Alas! They shout
He's fallen off with a clout
My Lord! They cry
Surely he is going to die!

A scramble of people, horses & men

Surely a hand I can now lend

Run down quickly

Round up the cavalry

Spook them to stand in line

For it is now time

To march on straight

Towards the gate

Carry him carefully

For he holds on sparingly

To a life that was whole

But now seemingly does fold

Stand back up with the birds and sing

As we all salute the king!

Humpty Dumpty

(Second person)

So it was you sitting up there in the tree

Looking so happy, merry and free

I saw you running around

Scurrying all around the ground

I saw you with such worry in your eye

I knew you wished you could jump up and fly

Like an eager beaver

Jumping and scurrying you did weaver

Amongst the Kings horses and men

A helpful hand you sure did lend

Spooking the horses back around the bend

To stand before the King in the hope he may mend

It was you Mr Squirrel sitting next to me in the tree

Merry, happily singing with glee.

Humpty Dumpty

(Third person)

Hush hush a story to be told
Allow me to tell you how it all did unfold

On this dark and stormy day
A man sat on a wall did give way
He splatted to the ground
People then scurrying all around

Chaos and shouting
People were bellowing and clouting
Hands raised in the air
Oh my God such despair

Horses in flight

From such fright

A little squirrel seemed to have the clue

He knew just what to do

He scurried down from a tree

Oh he did with such glee

From sitting and singing

He was now springing

Up and down

And all around

Spooking the horses and rallying them

Making them come back around the bend

He got them standing straight and tall

Right up along a wall

Suddenly there was a hush

No longer a mad rush

Men and horses once in flight

Now silent and standing in the light

Of day, all now walking away

With the King

In hand

Back to his land

Happy Days

I am sailing upon a sea

Oh is that buzz a honeybee?

No, it's a bird in flight

Flapping away from the night

Fish flurrying slashing in the water

Above a flight – is that a charter?

An osprey stalking

Seagulls chortling

A Story to Be Told

Items – Bubble Wrap, Preserving Jar,
Ancient Cave Man Painting

Bibbity bobbity boo

Ha ha I'm a jam jar too!

Hey hey

What did you say?

Pop pop pop

Over and over I flop

Ha ha, just like you

I can preserve too!

Excuse me Dears, you both so jolly

Dare anyone cast me a worry?

Ancient I am in deed

And great care do I need

For if you over me do flop

Or careless hands over me just drop

Then shall I fade

And distant conversations cascade

Far from dark or light

No one ever to hear our plight

Of oh what was such a fight

That one long day and night

Animals from far and wide

Did us threaten from the inside

Never such a war did you see

Between man and beast on a tee

Oh what a story to be told

Of a tale that did unfold

All captured now on a stone

If not done, it would be unknown

So Mr Bubble and Mrs Flop

Please would you be so kind

To keep me in mind

Tenderly wrap your arms around me

And keep me safe

From all dust and harm

And place me in your firm embrace

And sit me in a high place

Where all can see

And admire me

Disturbed Silence

From the songs out of the plane
Does anything ever remain the same?
From birds that flew around at night
Now take flight at morning light

Trains, cars and planes
Now all just remains
A look, a gasp
Oh what a contrast

Sirens break out in loud song
Silence broken for now so long
Gone are the birds of the night
Gone are the sounds at morning light

Busyness reigns

Everything now stained

With pompous, bold and vandalous life anew

Who would have ever knew

Of what came before

This life that's now afore

Nothing backward

Nothing lacking

Everything instant

Everything distant

Out of reach

Out of touch

Oh why is life such a rush?

Autumn

Shorter days this season displays

Cold and ice not quite so nice

Warm stews my Mom brews

The morning fog blurs eyes

The evening chill not quite so dill

Daylight sun not so fun

Then you often stand still

And so do cars in autumn chill

Can we have some quill?

The Telephone

I called him one day on the phone
Was it his voice or just a drone?
For so long I waited for this day
Since he left for far away

Up upon the train we said goodbye
How in my heart I felt I would die
From the hurt and pain
Of the love drain

Did I hear you say my name?
Oh but my love, it doesn't sound the same
Is it the time and space divide?
For it's since so long that I've been at your side

Oh my love, I still feel so strong

The love I have for you, even though it's been so long

So many months have passed

My love for you forever will last

Oh my love can we meet again?

Can we run around so freely like we had no pain?

My love, come back to me

My love – just you and me

My love, let's not be apart

For you have my whole heart

My love come back to me

My love, let's be for all eternity

May Day

On the first day of May
The sky turned blue
Oh what a sunny day
For me and you

Oh goodness my dear
Look at the sky above
Oh don't be filled with fear
It's a sign of God's love

It's a sign of promise
And not of pain
A sign of solace
For all of mankind's gain

Hush as we look up at the sky

The sound of rain is nearby

Blue! Its blue I say

Look as it falls this summery day

Oh it's gushing down today

Oh, it squashes all on its way

Goodness it falls so fast

How long will these flowers last?

Look as the new buds warily stand so strong

Oh for just how long

Can they keep their heads so high?

Against this rainy blue May sky?

Walking Through a City

About turn

Watch it burn

Wow a fire!

My God it's dire

Crunch crunch crunch

My eyes do bunch

At the sight of the flames

As they rage on and maim

All things in sight

Of this once great plight

That men worked for through the night

To build through the fight

Of mud and mire,

But it was not all dire

When men and squires

From far and wide

Would come and bide

In what once was a perch

But on then was built a church

Oh what a shame

As all seems lost

And what a shame

As it came at such a cost

Me and You Should Never Be Apart

To me and you

Oh how do you do?

A sigh, a name

What's your claim to fame?

My name my dear

Is have no fear

To all who believe

I bring relief

Of every lifelong pain

That has no gain

Open your heart

For us to never be apart

A Life So Free

The story of my life

Is one of strife

But also of joy and gain

From enduring pain

Not all is lost

From the cost

Be Bee Be

Like a bumblebee

Oh I am so free

Filled with glee

Hee hee hee!

Swirling and twirling

Buzzing and curling

Oh be like me

So free!

Roof Top Songs

Every roof top sings a song

Let's listen as we go along…

Birds chirping

Raindrops falling

Dew crawling

Ice crackling

Berries bouncing

Leaves sliding

Summer subsiding

All fall down but not like a clown

Everything rhymes, songs in time

From roof tops sing

Listen…listen to everything

And join in and sing

What I Really Dislike

Tomáto, tomàto

Potáto, potàto

Gráss, gràss

Báth, bath

What does it matter in the end?

People comparing

People staring

Sitting and glaring

Not even being daring

No-one caring

What is the point of your life my dear?

Sniggering, triggering

Belligerently buggering

A life so rife

Of disgusting, vile strife

I like the simple things in life

Peace and quiet

Still and silence

Love and laughter

The forever after

Friendship

Trust

Keep them a must

No pain

No strain

Happiness

Joy

Sailing on…ahoy

On a journey I go…oh boy

To let it all go

Let it all drop deep down to the big blue below…

Shine a Light

Happiness and pain

Sounds like a lot of strain

So far apart

Both lie deep in the heart

Tugging

Pulling

Worlds apart

Painful

Joyful

Less please

More please

No thanks

But yes thanks

Painfully growing

Through storms of life

Happily glowing

Through the breaks from life

Shine a light

Snuff the pain

Remove

Replace

Move on with grace

Graciously embrace

These aspects of life

To lessen the strife

And make the most of this precious life

Wasted Wealth

Sizzling sausages scream out a name

Please pick me promptly Mr Fame!

Bursting bubbling breaking out the flames

Desperately dancing dying in shame

Burning black before eyes in aim

What and why are you wasting my name?

Tantalizingly tasty to consume is my claim

Now witheringly wasting willinglessly ashamed

Broken in bits and now based to the frame

Of the beautiful brass blasted pan in this flame

Carelessly and callously cast away all blame

By hilariously harsh humans that exclaim

To be the best, better than the rest in their mortal frame

A wasted waste of wealth unclaimed

Together We Can

People passing everywhere

Does anyone stop to even give a care?

A pose

A rose

Does everyone have to be so flipping closed?

STOP!

PLOP!

Someone just dropped!

Did you see

Do you care?

Would you even dare?

Or will you just sit there and stare?

Round up three four

Up to the tee

And off the floor

Up up we go

Let's not lay down so low

Feelers out

Let's give this life a clout

Bellow out and let's stand tall

Together let's give this life our all

A helping hand

To walk together across this land

This terrain that's often filled with strife and pain

With great loss and little gain

Humans we are and humans we can be

Drop who and what is right, let go of all that's steely

Let us stand side by side

Let peace be our guide

And with one another humbly abide

A Love Gone Cold

Red is the colour blue

Especially when I'm thinking of you

Blue is the colour purple

As our love has gone cold like a turtle

Paled into insignificance

Is this once colourful romance

Of vibrant colours

That flowed as we loved each other

Blue replaces red

As I am lying here on my bed

A rose you were

A thorn you now are

Pink I was before

Now brown as I lay on my floor

Tears of a once golden glow

Now colourlessly and endlessly do flow

She Lives On Though She Has Gone

In the darkest night

There came a light

On that day

That all was taken away

Desperately I searched

From deep within the lurch

Of the abyss of pain

Scouring for what gain

Silenced…

Broken…

Unspoken…

Alone…

A wave of love

Filled from above

An angel of light

Fluttered in the night

A kiss of life she bought

Alongside me she fought

Strengthening me each day

Cheering me on my way

A true angel of light

Flew by that dark night

She watches over me still

Helping my life to be full

Mom

Oh Happy Day

Oh happy day

Oh happy daayy

Jesus washed

All my sins away

He hung named

Upon that cross

For all to see

For my wrongs

And yours too

As his eyes shut

So did the

Light of day

As this display

Of love showed

As daylight closed

Night time came
New day dawned
New life spawned

Free now we are
Free now we be
Darkness now
Became light

Mixed Morning

A dull and dusted misty morning
It's said a brand new year's day is dawning
I can't but help to bow my head as this is boring
These endless bouts of grey do keep me yawning

Hop up dear girl this is a brand new day
So many good things can come your way
Look up above go on your knees and pray
There is more often and always a way

Opportunities are there my dear
Rise up and boldly face your fear

Mr Fish

The fish swam up the stream

And with glee when he saw me

With a smile on his dial

Glad all the while

He drunk all the waste

Oh what a bad taste

Of gunk and dirt

No more could he flirt

With the rest in the sea

All he could do was now

Watch and see

Up From the Soil

I am a red tulip
And oh I stand so tall
People often watch me
Even when I fall

Long before I bloom
In the dark of winter
In the depth of the gloom
I'm carefully buried
In the richest of soils
Left unattended
And myself to fend

Through the coldest times
And sternly I survive

And as the seasons start to turn
Up from the soil I begin to churn

Slowly and steadily begin to flourish
And that without very little nourish

Bright and red I stand so tall
Soon I will fall

Look close and admire me
For not much longer of my glee

My Struggle

I'm grateful for the pain

For without it I would not know such gain

Like a bird in flight

She sweeps through the night

Only to hold on and fight

Until darkness turns light

Be still my soul

Causing so much pain

Oh what could be my gain?

Is it just me on my own

How could I be so alone

For I lived to give

Now I have to hold on through a sieve

No trickle of light

So I give up the fight

For My Mom on Her Birthday

If I were to have one wish for today
It would be that in my life you would stay
Not just fond memories of us two
But the living, real you

If I were to have one wish for today
It would be that you were not so far away
But right here by my side
Loving and guiding me against the tide

The tides of life
That bring so much strife
But with you by my side
I would have strength from the inside

To fight and stand strong

Through many a day that seemed too long

Too soon you were gone

Too soon I say

Oh what I would do for just one more day

To love on you

And do all the things you love

Now I have to wish them to you on the wings of a dove

Oh Mum

I just want to hear your voice

If only I were to have the choice

To keep you here

I ask myself why

But then I begin to cry

Why dear God

Oh why

She was the most beautiful soul

Did you need her more than me?

For surely you can see

That I need her here to be

Dear God

I wish my wish would come true

Even for just one day

So in my arms she could stay

If I had one wish for today

It would be to hold you in my arms

Dearest Mum

And sing to you happy birthday

No Body, No Pain

We only have today

Well, that's what they say

A day?

What is that anyway?

Are you sure?

Can you see

What it is really like for me?

Or only what it is like for thee...

Not to worry

I won't bother

Or trouble thee

It's only little unworthy me

Heaven's Gain

One day I will be heaven's gain

Oh what a day

When I will be away

From this pain inside

Nowhere will I have to hide

No pain

And oh what a gain

For I shall be truly home again ☺

Magnificent Mountains

Oh these magnificent mountains!

What is it you can see?

Birthing rivers and fountains

Bringing to life the sea

How mighty you stand

In you all life is preserved

Built from solid rock, not sand

In awe all stand back and observe

Your beauty and grace

Your endless faceted face

Your stalwart strength

Your height, your depth, your length

Oh magnificent mountains

How great you are indeed

All life from you is formed

In you all life is firmly held

Forever may you stand

Withstanding every element

That would seek to bring you down

Oh mountains keep standing strong

Oh mountains keep keeping us for long and forever

The Deep Secret

There is a river that runs night

It can be seen from way up high

The depths of its secrets remain unknown

Untold by the birds over which have flown

Untold by the centuries of rocks

Formed from within its locks

Untold by the greenery

Birthed by it to form this epic scenery

This 'source of life'

Has brought much strife

Of toils and war

Dividing nations afore

For boundaries sought
The wars were fought
Now an empire stands tall
Within which many did fall

Fall prey to the evil grasp
Of the never never kings gasp
To keep people near
Out of lonely fear

A seemingly stalwart throne he built
But fraught with lies and deception inbuilt
Unfathomable falseness from walls to the ground
Immense unhappiness within its walls found

Outwardly attractive
Inwardly distractive
From all forms of human life
Enter in and endure endless strife

Delight Land

She stood alone on white land
Once dark but now such light land

Sinking she felt very lost
Once bright but now dark night land

She tried to stand strong and tall
But ended in respite land

For all her life filled with strife
She imagined no bright land

Would ever help Rosie's plight
To arrive in delight land.

Night

I wish it were night all over again

Where the world sits still

In a quiet chill

Where hustle and bustle ceases

And peace and tranquil increases

I wish it were night all over again

I wish it were night

What a Day

There's someone in heaven
Who I wish was here today
She's been there for so long
And is so far away

There is someone in heaven
Who I would do anything to see
She brought me up
And helped me be all that I can be

There is someone in heaven
Who I long for everyday
Please God keep her safe
Until I go through heavens gates

What a day that will be

To live with her for all eternity

In Peace

If I fought hard could I die in peace?
Would it be a sin to lie in peace?

The world would say run hard, run faster
My mind says it's time to fly in peace

Fly to a world above this dark world
Where serene sounds leave you high in peace

Where lofty falls of rivers flowing
Bring life, love from wishful skies in peace
If I fought hard, would you allow me to rest?
Or let me slip away high in peace?

Family

When you're around

It feels like my feet are on solid ground

Old life within me is found

The inside of me is bouncing around

When you're around my life is lighter

May days are so much brighter

I don't have to be so much of a fighter

I feel I can hold onto life a lot tighter

When you're around my poorly body feels more strong

My days feel less long

I feel I belong

The inside of me hums a constant happy song

Those We Love

When those we love go away

Lots of them does stay

Physically here no more

But memories, love, a life lived

With us evermore do stay

Gone from the earth they are

But from us not far

For all they taught us

And all they were

Remains in us and part of us

And will always live on through us

*I T*ried

I tried to connect with you

I really did

Some slight sparkles but it seems you went and hid

Despite all the things for you I did

You've gone and hid

I was important when I could function

Now I can't I'm left at a junction

Of loneliness and despair without you there

Promises of good times ahead

Unfulfilled leaving me bereft in my bed

I tried to connect with you, I really did

I can't think why you went and hid

I ask myself what wrong did I do
Is it me or is it you
I'm not sure I have the clue
But I know my love for you was strong
That's what kept my hope up for so long
I tried to connect with you I really did

I still can't think of why you went and hid

My worth from God I've delved to find
For if it was sought in mankind
I would be nothing but a piece of dirt
Lost in a gigantic rubbish tip

I tried to connect with you I really did
For my sanity from you I've now hid

Mom in Heaven

Happy birthday to my mom in Heaven

Longingly I look into the endless sky

Wishing that you did not die

Wishing I could see your beautiful face

And be in the warmth of your loving embrace

Days and years go by

But every day my heart still cries

For from you I came

And through you I became

All that I am is because of you

What you taught me now sees me through

Not You, Not Me

I don't know if I can describe

The loneliness I feel inside

These conditions encapsulate me

And have taken away all I wanted to be

I don't know if I could tell you about my days

For how I could describe in simple ways

The strife

The pain

For if I tell you, what will I gain?

Only to be repeating my hell again and again

Shove it away!

Don't let it see the light of day

Lock it away deep inside

For it is there with it you hide

For fear of allowing

Yourself to start crying

Don't let anyone know!

For surely you cannot show

The vast divide

From within you and what shows on the outside

Sshh….

Don't say a word

Let nothing be heard

No pain

No gain

Or shall I just let myself wane

Along with all the pain

Stay calm

Be strong

Oh really?

Just for how long?

Let the birds carry on in song
Let the days be happy and long
For those free and sane
And know not real pain

Carry on into the night
Happy, singing take flight
Be free
Be all you can be
And…don't worry about me.

A New Season

Flowers springing blossoming and blooming

Birds fluttering and bees buzzing insects singing

All dancing in spring sunshine

A New Day

A new day dawning

Spring springing joyful singing

Dancing in the sun

As We Are

From darkness to dust

Whirling words creating life

Onwards flowing life

Time

Time started from one word

Creation flourishing, flashfully, blissfully and effortlessly flowing

Gift of life all enjoying

The Still

Icy brown grass

Steamy dull sky lines

Heavy breathing

Falling Silence

Trees turning

Log fires burning

Silence starts to fall

Happy Days

Springing flowers

Aboundingly blooming

Bees buzzing

Sweets

Juicy succulent

Tantalisingly express

Taste buds from under duress

The Last Day

Heaven's angels call

All flooding in to the king

Repentant heads bowed

Snowflakes

Softly, skilfully slowly showering down

Faithfully and frillfully flurries flowing heavily upon

Tiredly torn tainted planet earth

The Town

A town with a name

Oh does anything ever stay the same?

Nottingham?

Or Shottingham?

Who on earth is to blame?

Gunshots and fires burning

History falling and marsh grounds turning

Riots and shouting

Silence ablaze old woodens clouting

Smashing and clashing

Breaking and bashing

History across time

To make this town now mine

For centuries the unawoken

Of the town is yet to be spoke

Silently kept secrets

Hidden promises

Plans yet to unfold once found

In the history of this supposedly known town

Tired

Slap me in the face

And knock me to the floor

I'm tired of this phase

And now I say no more

Reject me again and again

I can no longer take this pain

My feelings matter to you no more

As I lay here shaking on the floor

Crap on me

Make me to look like shit

For to you I am just a squirt

A blurt, a vapour

Easily snuffed out and wiped away

Every good I did for you

Now nothing from you ensues

All in vain

I endured such pain

Misfits

She tried and tried and tried

But then she cried out aloud

My God why does it have to be so hard?!

She feels like a big fat piece of lard

Her heart so tender

Does anyone render

Just a thought or a smile

Is she really not worthwhile?

A blast from the past

Was she ever going to last?

Her time here on earth

Struck down not long after her birth

Rejected she's been indeed
Her needs made to look like greeds

Ha ha! They say
Look at her as she goes on her way!

A bloody fool she is for sure
Knock her for good to the floor
Make sure she is no more
One…two…THREE…FOUR…

She turns her back
Waiting for the almighty whack
Lifeless she fights not
Against the perilous lot

To her knees she falls
Her world folded
Eyes shut
She waits…

Silence

A hush of wind

A sheep bleating

A duck quacking

Birds singing

Trees waving

Earthworms churning

Water flowing

Silently she waits in nature's arms

Gingerly embracing all that brings her no harm

Her body slumped on fertile ground

Her soul smiling as she has now been found

From the dirt she was created

Now it is keeping her placated

Peace from deep within

Her deep belonging she has found

A Formed Life

Bones at the bottom of the sea

What on earth could they be?

They elegantly lie there with a sense of glee

For they became from you to me

From ashes to dust

They became a must

A must that was built from trust

And not out of lust

For your life to be formed

Each stage needs to be transformed

From ashes to dust

You became a must

Breath I breathed into your lungs

Eyes I formed for you to see

Ears I formed for you to hear

Limbs I formed for you to use

From ashes to dust

You became a must

A soul she now has

A heart with which she can feel

A life she has indeed

Walking, running, her inner self now freed

From ashes to dust

She became a must

A must that was built on trust

And out of pure love, not lust

His life through hers continually flows

Bringing light and love wherever she goes

From ashes to dust

She became a must

A force she is to be reckoned with indeed

Spending her life, helping others in need

Never stopping, always giving

Her life fully living

From ashes to dust

She is now a must

Angel of Light

Like an angel of light
She came to me on that night
The night I drifted so far away
She came to stay

Life ringing all around
On my new trepardous ground
Full of beans
Bringing me all that life means

She was an angel of light
To me on that night
Stripped of all that was there
I felt naked and bare

She comforted me

And helped me

Bringing me solace

And every kind of grace

Showing no fear on her face

She comforted me with a smiling embrace

An angel of light

Came to me on that night

Such warmth from within

My chances of finding this love so slim

Loving kindness exuding from all her being

Helping me to stop fleeing

From an internal flight

Filled with fear from that night

My angel of light

Oh so bright

God bless her soul

And always keep her well

The Rose

A buzzing bee I am indeed
Fluttering around to those in need
Those who've opened up from tight and small
Who have grown up so big and tall

Those who call themselves roses
Those who are not just for posers
Rather to tickle the senses of people's noses
Painfully pruned for sure
Never are we chucked ashore

For romance we are well used
Memorable occasions we adorn
Promises of summers we strive to show
Strong and tall we stand aglow

Bringing many a smile

Lasting a long while

Mothers favourites we are for sure

We just keep growing more and more

So Beautiful To Me

She was so beautiful to me
She was so beautiful to me
She came in like the morning sun
Helped me from my fears not to run

Her beauty so clearly displayed
In every single one of her ways
Her sincerity for me so strong
Helping my many dark days along

Helping me to stand and fight
Through many a dark and terror full night
Always shining such light
Upon my stark and lonely plight

Radiance and hope

A fresh and beautiful breeze

A beacon

A strong tower

A safe embrace

An ever smiling face

Unending wisdom

Unending care

Was always with her there

Could I begin to dare

To lower my walls bare

To breathe in such love and care

When life has been an awful snare

A snowdrop opened

And closed again

And opened

And closed again

And opened....

Her tender love it held

And slowly closed again

She was so beautiful to me

She was so beautiful to me

As You Sleep

My prayer for you before you sleep tonight
Is that you feel Him holding you tight
That you feel safe in His embrace
And your feet firm in a safe place

My prayer for you before you sleep tonight
Is that you will know just how much you're loved
How much you're appreciated
And how much you're adored

My prayer for you before you sleep tonight
Is that all pain, worry and care
Will be laid at His feet
And warmth and love your heart does greet

My prayer for you just as you fall asleep tonight
Is that you will feel whole, loved and His light
And love shining upon you His precious child

May you feel His smile upon your life
And His warmth in your heart and body

My prayer for you as you sleep tonight
Is that His love may saturate your heart
All pain be gently washed away
Wounds of the past wholly healed
And His love in your heart forever sealed

Sleep in heavenly peace

Onwards You Go

My Darling Daughter

Always be yourself as they say

But don't be too proud

Carefully think about your future

Desire to achieve high

Excel with your God-given gifts

Foster love and kindness in your every step

Go for your dreams with all your heart

Happiness happens in the smallest of things

Insight will be your best friend

Joy can be found in your every day

Keep keeping on even when your strength has gone

Love people, love God, love life

Make the most of every situation

No-one can put you down except yourself

Operate with kindness in everything

People come, people go – but don't let it break you

Quiet your soul at the start of each day

Remind yourself always that everything will be okay

Stand tall with all of who you are

Try your hardest in everything – it will pay off I promise

Understand where people are coming from and why

Voice your opinion when the time is right

Wonder, dream and never stop

Xylophones, guitars and instruments can calm the soul

Zeal, my darling, zeal – let it consume the whole of you, never let anyone take it from you and never let it go.

All my love and God be with you

Mum

Your Light

When the days get darker

And the nights get longer

When tough times get tougher

And your resting place gets rougher

When the hope you had has gone

And the light you saw is darkness.

Walk on my friend. Walk on.

Look forward when you cannot see

Walk even though you're completely broken.

Breathe even though it hurts so much.

Walk on my friend.

Walk on.

Your light will come.

Printed in Great Britain
by Amazon